Empathic Mastery Diary

This journal belongs to

Name

Email

+ ( ) -

© 2023, 2024 (Revised Edition) Jennifer Elizabeth Moore all rights reserved.

This diary or parts thereof may not be reproduced in any form, stored in any retrieval system, or transmitted in any form by any means—electronic, mechanical, photocopy, recording, or otherwise—without prior written permission of the publisher, except in the case of brief quotations embodied in critical reviews and certain other noncommercial uses permitted by United States of America copyright law.
For permission requests, write to the publisher at the address below.

Modern Medicine Lady LLC
P.O. Box 93 Pownal, ME 04069 USA
attn: Permissions Coordinator

Book Design, & Cover Image
by Jennifer E Moore
Printed by Jennifer Elizabeth Moore in Pownal, ME in the USA
First Printing Edition 2023 Des'Tai Press
Second Printing Edition 2024 Des'Tai Press

ISBN: 978-1-950984-06-0 (Paperback) (B&W interior)
ISBN: 978-1-950984-07-7 (Hardcover) (Color interior)

Although the author and publisher have made every effort to ensure that the information in this book was correct at press time, the author and publisher do not assume and hereby disclaim any liability to any party for any loss, damage, or disruption caused by errors or omissions, whether such errors or omissions result from negligence, accident, or any other cause. Because of the dynamic nature of the Internet, any web addresses or links contained in this book may have changed since publication of this book and may no longer be valid.

The opinions and information shared in this journal are based on the experience, teachings and creative inspiration of the author. Your mileage may vary. Please take what you like and leave the rest. This guide is not intended as a substitute for the medical advice of a licensed healthcare provider. The reader should consult a qualified medical professional in matters relating to her/his mental and physical health and particularly with respect to any symptoms that may require diagnosis or medical attention. The intent of the author is to share information to support you in your pursuit of empathic, emotional and spiritual wellness.

In the event that you use any of the information in this book for yourself or anyone else, the author and publisher assume no responsibility for your choices and actions.

For more information visit EmpathicMastery.com

"Know Thyself" are the words inscribed at the historic Temple of Apollo in Delphi. The ancient Greeks visited this temple to receive guidance, clarity and Divine Wisdom. All were greeted by this motto. It reminds us that intuition begins with self knowledge.

There's an interesting balance between intuition and self knowledge. Essentially, the more we know ourselves, the more accurate our intuition is. However, when we can't recognize what's making us tick, we mistake triggers for intuition or premonitions. When we're caught up in empathic overwhelm it's easy to perceive emotional intensity as inner guidance. We can also interpret psychic hits and flashes as different from what they actually represent. Therefore, when it comes to developing intuition, before we can dive into opening our channel we need to know ourselves and learn to discern what's ours and what isn't.

The foundation of well-honed intuitive ability lies in understanding ourselves. When we establish the baseline for our own thoughts, feelings and sensations, we can identify what's going on within and beyond ourselves. It becomes much easier to discern what's happening when we're aware of what is occurring internally as well as around us.

This diary takes the principles of Empathic Mastery and provides a space for you to work with them as an ongoing practice. It's my sincere hope that with regular journaling you'll access the inner wisdom that reveals a path to your best possibilities. I hold the vision that 13 moons from now, you'll be able to celebrate shifts that have allowed you to align with the success, abundance and delicious fulfillment that your dear empath soul desires.

xoxo Jen

How to Use This Book

I've configured this diary so you can begin tracking anytime during the year around a new moon. But first, take time to work on the initial pages regardless of the moon phase. This section helps you to establish your baseline. First, to clarify your deepest heart's desires. Next, to express how you'd like to think, act, and feel. Then, to determine what you wish to manifest, whom you hope to be, and what you desire to impact.

Part two is structured to guide and support you through the thirteen moon cycles of an entire year. You might start on the new moon at the beginning of the year, around the launch of a project, near your birthday, or any other significant event. Each moon cycle section contains weekly pages for the four major lunar phases. Start on the first day of the moon cycle. This amounts to the 52 weeks of an entire calendar year. Each of the thirteen sections contains five aspects. The first segment presents an affirmation that you can use as a focus for the following four weeks. The second is designed to help you define your current reality through observation of your inner and outer world. The third provides pages for monthly discoveries, truth, and wisdom. It includes a page to journal on the five steps of Empathic Mastery: RECOGNIZE, RELEASE, PROTECT, CONNECT and ACT. These pages give you space to acknowledge your truth and anchor your intentions. The fourth segment is where you'll make daily and weekly notes. Unlike a blank journal, where you might write multiple pages every day, these pages are designed to capture the essence by using keywords and brief phrases. The fifth section is where you'll claim your wins, acknowledge your revelations, and make observations. Finally, at the end of the diary is a place to review your year and celebrate your victories, lessons, and shifts. It's also where you can begin to imagine the possibilities for your next year. I believe that when you use this journal consistently for an entire year, you'll deepen your self awareness. This ongoing exploration will help to enhance your intuition and support your intentions.

Get the Most Bang for Your Buck

OVERWHELM! It's the thing that stops so many of us in our tracks. Add empathic worry and stress to the mix, and our mental, emotional and energetic bandwidth becomes really narrow. Sometimes we have the motivation, energy and resources to commit to the whole shebang; other times focusing on the bare minimum is more than enough. In the case of this diary, my hope is that you'll use it in the way that works best for you.

As you peruse this volume, you'll discover there are sections for annual, monthly, weekly, and daily journaling. The monthly pages help you to define and notice the shifts in your baselines. They'll also help you to feel more present, grounded and embodied. You may wish to set aside a special time near the new moon (or at any time that serves you) for these entries. However, you can also work with this section whenever you need to recalibrate and remember your place in the Universe. This approach is especially helpful when you're feeling dysregulated, anxious or ungrounded.

Weekly pages provide space to set intentions to begin your week and record your results at the end of it. You may wish to do this every week. You may find it more aligned to do these pages only when you feel called to them. The daily sections on My Wonderful Week help to process your day. Out of everything in this diary, I encourage you to commit to filling out these brief but powerful daily reviews. These entries will take no more than a few minutes every day. If you can brush your teeth daily, you can do this. If you have just a bit more bandwidth, I invite you to carve out 10-30 minutes at the beginning of your week to plan ahead and use the Anchoring Intentions section. How you use this diary is ultimately up to you. Only you know whether you do better with routines and established habits, by taking a more spontaneous approach, or something with a bit of both.

Working with the Moon

When you consider how profoundly the moon influences ocean tides, it's easy to imagine that our brains, which are composed of 80-85% water, are affected too. Humans have coordinated their plans with lunar cycles from the dawn of our existence as a species. When we align with this rhythm, our connection and flow with the Universe are amplified.

Moon Phases

New Moon: set intentions, plant seeds, call in dreams, & launch projects
Waxing Moon: identify needs, water seeds, nurture growth, & tend projects
Full Moon: amplify intentions, celebrate growth, make offerings, & give thanks
Waning Moon: take inventory, prune dead weight, release, & purify

Every moon cycle moves through all 12 of the zodiac signs. The new moon is always in the same sign as the sun. For example, if it's Leo season, then the new moon will also be in Leo. The full moon is always in the sign opposite to the sun. So when the sun is in Capricorn, the full moon is in Cancer.

Moons in Zodiac Signs

Each zodiac sign correlates with one of the four elements.
Air Moons – Gemini, Libra & Aquarius: For mindset, writing, ideas & inspiration, developing plans, & other mental endeavors.
Fire Moons – Aries, Leo & Sagittarius: For taking action, starting adventures, building momentum, breaking habits, & shifting behaviors.
Water Moons – Cancer, Scorpio & Pisces: For matters of the heart, accessing dreams & intuition, releasing wounds, & other emotional work.
Earth Moons – Taurus, Virgo & Capricorn: For financial ventures, crafting, creating things, addressing health, & physical manifestation.

While it may be fairly easy to recall the sign of every new and full moon, it takes more effort to determine exact times and the phases in between. For this I recommend using a phone app to track the moons with precise detail. Of the ones I've tried, iLuna is my personal favorite. It's easy to use with monthly & daily views.

Anchoring Habits

Starting anything new takes effort. Even when we desire results and feel motivated, it's easy to get derailed. Here are a few hacks I've discovered that increase our chances for success.

- Get clear on your WHY. Imagine the outcome you desire. Write down your vision and the reasons why this matters to you.
- Claim space and time to do the work. You've probably heard a variation of Benjamin Franklin's old chestnut: "By failing to plan, you are preparing to fail." Instead of either waiting for the perfect moment to reveal itself, or leaving it all up to chance, you'll get way further by scheduling regular monthly, weekly, and daily blocks in your calendar.
- Consider your days, weeks and months to find already established routines or habits that you can "graft" these new behaviors onto. For example, if you always prepare a morning beverage and pause to drink it while you check email or social media, start with journaling for 5-10 minutes. Then reward your effort with the dopamine hit you get from scrolling your phone.
- Take small, incremental steps instead of trying to change everything at once. Allow yourself to anchor the step and then add the next. Be honest with yourself about what you can realistically accomplish. It's far better to maintain one small habit with consistency than to be overly ambitious and drop the ball after only a few days or weeks.

Keep It Simple

While you'll find pages in this diary for notes, most of it has been formatted for keywords, bullet points and a phrase or two. Think haiku, instead of novel. Avoid head stories. Follow your heart's truth. Distill each entry to its essence. Focus on the core, the kernel, the bottom line. Take a moment to breathe in your connection to Divine Source. Ground and center yourself. Consider the writing prompt and then go with the first answer you receive. Don't overthink it or worry about being right. Inner wisdom comes in an instant. Trust the still, small voice within.

The 5 Steps of Empathic Mastery

Let's start with my definition of "empath." An empath is a highly sensitive being who picks up and absorbs thoughts, emotions, sensations and energy from the world around them. However, where intuitives, psychics, and mediums can usually distinguish what's theirs and what's coming from outside themselves, empaths process what they receive as if it's theirs. This is one of the reasons being an empath can be challenging. Over the course of a few decades, I've come to understand that we need more than a bubble of light and a few well-placed affirmations to become empowered empaths. Through a lot of trial and error, hitting walls, and pivoting, my five step system unfolded for me.

RECOGNIZE, RELEASE, PROTECT, CONNECT and ACT. They work as both a multi-step system and as individual tools. This diary has been created to support your awareness of all of them. At first, we work incrementally. It might take hours, days, weeks, months or even years to explore and fully integrate one step. However, after practice these steps become a process you can use to shift from empathic overwhelm to access your gifts and realize your life's purpose.

- RECOGNIZE: First, we recognize ourselves as highly sensitive empaths and identify the unique care we need. Next, we define our baseline so we can discern when we are feeling out of sorts or picking up unexplainable distress. Then we work to recognize what's ours and what isn't. Finally, we examine the what, where, and why so we can address and shift whatever needs attention. To begin, place your hands over your heart and ask yourself "Is this mine?" Notice your immediate response.

- RELEASE: Once we recognize we've taken on energy that isn't ours or that our own triggers, limiting beliefs, or patterns of imbalance were activated, we work to release what no longer serves us. There are many ways to do this. Decluttering, detoxing, and EFT/tapping are a few. I go into detail with techniques and tools in my book, _Empathic Mastery_. One of my favorites uses mindful breathing. I tune in to my core. I inhale calmness. Then, I state: "I release this to where it belongs" as I exhale.

PROTECT: This step follows RECOGNIZE and RELEASE because protection is most effective when we are not carrying empathic overwhelm, emotional distress, or unhealed inner wounds. This requires both energetic and strategic boundaries. On the energetic level, we cultivate or restore robust filters and shields. This helps with the empath's porous nature and vulnerability to external energy. On the strategic level, we set limits with our resources and what we are willing and not willing to do. This is where we define our terms and say no to misaligned requests and demands. I recorded a guided exercise to help you build up your filters and shields and to plug into the power source of the earth and sky. You can access this and additional tools by visiting EmpathicSafety.com

CONNECT: You've heard the saying the Universe abhors a vacuum? We must replace the stuff we've released with something more aligned and positive. This step is about establishing a connection with a power greater than ourselves and learning to access the Divine Wisdom that comes with it. How we define this Source is deeply personal. Only you get to decide with whom or what you have this relationship. We deepen this link through prayer, meditation, ritual, chanting, guided meditation, and other acts of devotion. The first three steps are about addressing our empathic sensitivity and establishing our equilibrium. CONNECT is where we deepen our intuitive awareness so we can find our path of ease, grace and flow.

ACT: Living an empowered life requires commitment to aligned action, integrity and personal responsibility. It's one thing to hope and dream. It's another to take the steps needed to serve our highest purpose and manifest our deepest heart's desire. This final step is about strategy, approach, and mindset. While ego-driven agendas are often about "crushing it" and upping our productivity, the Empathic Mastery way is as much about the behaviors and attitudes we abstain from as it is about the ones we engage in. Instead of focusing on the details – "I want a Lexus, to manifest 6 figures next quarter, to become a famous influencer with 7 million followers on IG" – we dial in what our optimal state of being feels like and use this as the GPS to guide us. With each choice or action we ask ourselves "does this support the quality of life I desire?"

Initial Questions

What is your biggest challenge as an empath or sensitive person?

How will you hold yourself accountable and what kind of resistance do you need to watch for?

What do you especially want to shift this year?

What do you hope to achieve by working with this diary?

Notes

Starting Baseline

Date ____/____/____

Gauge how you feel
-10 is the worst. +10 is the absolute best.

−10 ▮▮▮▮▮▮ **0** ▯▯▯▯▯▯ **+10**

1. Physical Wellbeing _____
2. Mental Wellbeing _____
3. Emotional Wellbeing _____
4. Spiritual Wellbeing _____
5. Alignment with Divine Source _____
6. Sleep & Relaxation _____
7. Sensitivities or Allergies _____
8. Financial Security _____
9. Confidence & Success _____
10. Vitality & Drive _____
11. Creative Expression _____
12. Intimate Relationships _____
13. Energetic Filters & Shields _____
14. Strategic Boundaries _____
15. Overwhelm _____
16. Taking On Other People's Thoughts/Feelings _____
17. Attraction to/from Wounded People _____
18. Urgent Need to Rescue _____
19. Awfulizing _____
20. Awareness of Ghosts & Spirits _____
21. Past Life Trauma _____
22. Ancestral Trauma _____

Total Score _____

Realizations & Insights

My Heart's Desire

What will bring you JOY? List your deepest desires & wildest dreams

My Intention for 13 Moons from Now

AIR: How I wish to THINK

_____
_____
_____
_____
_____

FIRE: How I wish to ACT

_____
_____
_____
_____
_____

WATER: How I wish to FEEL

_____
_____
_____
_____
_____

EARTH: What I wish to MANIFEST

_____
_____
_____
_____
_____

SPIRIT: Whom I wish to BE

SOUL: What I hope to IMPACT

13 Moons

My Empathic Mastery Journal

Moon 1

I can distinguish my thoughts and feelings from the rest of the world.

I discern what's mine and what isn't.

Environment

Date ____/____/____

Smell (close, nearby, faraway)

_____
_____
_____
_____

Sound (close, nearby, faraway)

_____
_____
_____
_____
_____
_____
_____
_____

Sight (close, nearby, faraway)

_____
_____
_____
_____
_____
_____
_____
_____
_____
_____

Touch (Surfaces & Textures around me)

_____
_____
_____

Body Scan

Date ____/____/____

How are your feeling? What are you noticing?

Head & Face

_____
_____
_____
_____

Neck & Shoulders

_____
_____
_____
_____

Spine

_____
_____
_____
_____

Hips & Buttocks

_____
_____
_____
_____

Pelvis & Groin

_____
_____
_____
_____

Chest, Lungs & Heart

_____
_____
_____
_____

Solar Plexus & Belly

_____
_____
_____
_____

Arms & Hands

_____
_____
_____
_____

Legs & Feet

_____
_____
_____
_____

Skin

_____
_____
_____
_____

Additional Notes

_____
_____
_____
_____
_____
_____
_____
_____

Sensation Awareness

Date ____/____/____

Gauge how you feel
-10 is the worst. +10 is the absolute best.

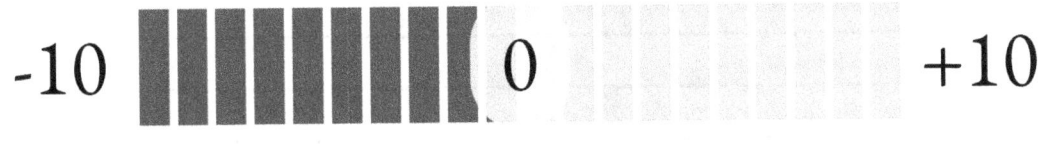

-10　　　　　　　　　　0　　　　　　　　　　+10

-_____ + **Temperature: Freezing - Sweltering**

_____
_____
_____
_____
_____

-_____ + **Density: Leaden - Weightless**

_____
_____
_____
_____
_____

-_____ + **Vibration/MPH: Still - Speed of Light**

_____
_____
_____
_____
_____

-_____ + **Energy: Lethargic - Invigorated**

_____
_____
_____
_____
_____

Observations
_____
_____
_____
_____
_____

Self Awareness

Date ____/____/____

In my Mind

_____
_____
_____
_____
_____
_____

In my Heart

_____
_____
_____
_____
_____
_____

From my Soul

_____
_____
_____
_____
_____
_____

Realizations

_____
_____
_____
_____
_____
_____
_____
_____

What I know to be True: Inner Wisdom

Anchoring Intentions

Plan your Weeks. What & How do you need to RECOGNIZE, RELEASE, PROTECT, CONNECT & ACT

Week 1: New Moon

To Recognize

To Release

To Protect

To Connect

To Act

Week 2: Waxing Moon

To Recognize

To Release

To Protect

To Connect

To Act

Week 3: Full Moon

To Recognize

To Release

To Protect

To Connect

To Act

Week 4: Waning Moon

To Recognize

To Release

To Protect

To Connect

To Act

My Priorities

My Wonderful Week   ___/___/___

Review your day. What's the takeaway? What are you integrating? What will you invite?

New Moon
Takeaway

Integrating

Invite

Waxing Crescent
Takeaway

Integrating

Invite

Waxing Crescent
Takeaway

Integrating

Invite

Waxing Crescent
Takeaway

Integrating

Invite

Waxing Crescent
Takeaway

Integrating

Invite

Waxing Crescent
Takeaway

Integrating

Invite

Waxing Crescent
Takeaway

Integrating

Invite

My Wonderful Week   ___/___/___

Review your day. What's the takeaway? What are you integrating? What will you invite?

First Quarter
Takeaway

Integrating

Invite

Waxing Gibbous
Takeaway

Integrating

Invite

Waxing Gibbous
Takeaway

Integrating

Invite

Waxing Gibbous
Takeaway

Integrating

Invite

Waxing Gibbous
Takeaway

Integrating

Invite

Waxing Gibbous
Takeaway

Integrating

Invite

Waxing Gibbous
Takeaway

Integrating

Invite

My Wonderful Week   ___/___/___

Review your day. What's the takeaway? What are you integrating? What will you invite?

Full Moon
Takeaway

Integrating

Invite

Waning Gibbous
Takeaway

Integrating

Invite

Waning Gibbous
Takeaway

Integrating

Invite

Waning Gibbous
Takeaway

Integrating

Invite

Waning Gibbous
Takeaway

Integrating

Invite

Waning Gibbous
Takeaway

Integrating

Invite

Waning Gibbous
Takeaway

Integrating

Invite

My Wonderful Week   ___/___/___

Review your day. What's the takeaway? What are you integrating? What will you invite?

Last Quarter
Takeaway
Integrating
Invite

Waning Crescent
Takeaway
Integrating
Invite

Waning Crescent
Takeaway
Integrating
Invite

Waning Crescent
Takeaway
Integrating
Invite

Waning Crescent
Takeaway
Integrating
Invite

Waning Crescent
Takeaway
Integrating
Invite

Dark Moon
Takeaway
Integrating
Invite

Celebrations & Miracles

Week 1: New Moon

_____
_____
_____
_____

Week 2: Waxing Moon

_____
_____
_____
_____

Week 3: Full Moon

_____
_____
_____
_____

Week 4: Waning Moon

_____
_____
_____
_____

Affirming Statement of Gratitude

_____
_____
_____

Observations & Realizations

Moon 2

I release any energy, emotions or beliefs that no longer serve me.

It's safe for me to let that stuff go.

Environment

Date ——/——/——

Smell (close, nearby, faraway)

_____
_____
_____

Sound (close, nearby, faraway)

_____
_____
_____
_____
_____
_____
_____

Sight (close, nearby, faraway)

_____
_____
_____
_____
_____
_____
_____
_____
_____

Touch (Surfaces & Textures around me)

_____
_____
_____
_____

Body Scan

Date ____/____/____

How are your feeling? What are you noticing?

Head & Face
_____
_____
_____

Neck & Shoulders
_____
_____
_____

Spine
_____
_____
_____

Hips & Buttocks
_____
_____
_____

Pelvis & Groin
_____
_____
_____

Chest, Lungs & Heart
_____
_____
_____

Solar Plexus & Belly
_____
_____
_____

Arms & Hands
_____
_____
_____

Legs & Feet
_____
_____
_____

Skin
_____
_____
_____

Additional Notes

_____
_____
_____
_____
_____
_____
_____
_____

Sensation Awareness

Date ____/____/____

Gauge how you feel
-10 is the worst. +10 is the absolute best.

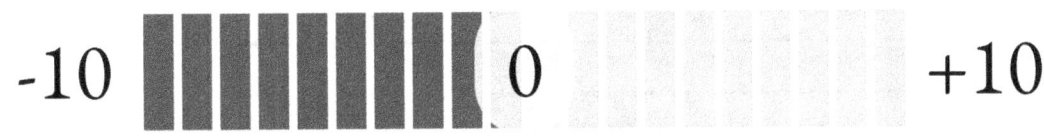

-_____+ Temperature: Freezing - Sweltering

-_____+ Density: Leaden - Weightless

-_____+ Vibration/MPH: Still - Speed of Light

-_____+ Energy: Lethargic - Invigorated

Observations

Self Awareness

Date ——/——/——

In my Mind

___

In my Heart

___

From my Soul

___

Realizations

___

What I know to be True: Inner Wisdom

Anchoring Intentions

Plan your Weeks. What & How do you need to RECOGNIZE, RELEASE, PROTECT, CONNECT & ACT

Week 1: New Moon

To Recognize

To Release

To Protect

To Connect

To Act

Week 2: Waxing Moon

To Recognize

To Release

To Protect

To Connect

To Act

Week 3: Full Moon

To Recognize

To Release

To Protect

To Connect

To Act

Week 4: Waning Moon

To Recognize

To Release

To Protect

To Connect

To Act

My Priorities

My Wonderful Week   / /

Review your day. What's the takeaway? What are you integrating? What will you invite?

New Moon
Takeaway

Integrating

Invite

Waxing Crescent
Takeaway

Integrating

Invite

Waxing Crescent
Takeaway

Integrating

Invite

Waxing Crescent
Takeaway

Integrating

Invite

Waxing Crescent
Takeaway

Integrating

Invite

Waxing Crescent
Takeaway

Integrating

Invite

Waxing Crescent
Takeaway

Integrating

Invite

My Wonderful Week   ___/___/___

Review your day. What's the takeaway? What are you integrating? What will you invite?

First Quarter
Takeaway

Integrating

Invite

Waxing Gibbous
Takeaway

Integrating

Invite

Waxing Gibbous
Takeaway

Integrating

Invite

Waxing Gibbous
Takeaway

Integrating

Invite

Waxing Gibbous
Takeaway

Integrating

Invite

Waxing Gibbous
Takeaway

Integrating

Invite

Waxing Gibbous
Takeaway

Integrating

Invite

My Wonderful Week ___/___/___

Review your day. What's the takeaway? What are you integrating? What will you invite?

Full Moon
Takeaway

Integrating

Invite

Waning Gibbous
Takeaway

Integrating

Invite

Waning Gibbous
Takeaway

Integrating

Invite

Waning Gibbous
Takeaway

Integrating

Invite

Waning Gibbous
Takeaway

Integrating

Invite

Waning Gibbous
Takeaway

Integrating

Invite

Waning Gibbous
Takeaway

Integrating

Invite

My Wonderful Week ___/___/___

Review your day. What's the takeaway? What are you integrating? What will you invite?

Last Quarter
Takeaway

Integrating

Invite

Waning Crescent
Takeaway

Integrating

Invite

Waning Crescent
Takeaway

Integrating

Invite

Waning Crescent
Takeaway

Integrating

Invite

Waning Crescent
Takeaway

Integrating

Invite

Waning Crescent
Takeaway

Integrating

Invite

Dark Moon
Takeaway

Integrating

Invite

Celebrations & Miracles

Week 1: New Moon

_____
_____
_____
_____

Week 2: Waxing Moon

_____
_____
_____
_____

Week 3: Full Moon

_____
_____
_____
_____

Week 4: Waning Moon

_____
_____
_____
_____

Affirming Statement of Gratitude

_____
_____
_____
_____

Observations & Realizations

Moon 3

I'm held, supported, and protected by the earth beneath me and the sky above me.

My roots go deep. I stand strong even in the midst of chaos.

Environment

Date ——/——/——

Smell (close, nearby, faraway)

_____
_____
_____

Sound (close, nearby, faraway)

_____
_____
_____
_____
_____
_____
_____

Sight (close, nearby, faraway)

_____
_____
_____
_____
_____
_____
_____
_____
_____

Touch (Surfaces & Textures around me)

_____
_____
_____
_____

Body Scan

Date ____/____/____

How are your feeling? What are you noticing?

Head & Face

_____
_____
_____

Neck & Shoulders

_____
_____
_____

Spine

_____
_____
_____

Hips & Buttocks

_____
_____
_____

Pelvis & Groin

_____
_____
_____

Chest, Lungs & Heart

_____
_____
_____

Solar Plexus & Belly

_____
_____
_____

Arms & Hands

_____
_____
_____

Legs & Feet

_____
_____
_____

Skin

_____
_____
_____

Additional Notes

_____
_____
_____
_____
_____
_____
_____

Sensation Awareness

Date ____/____/____

Gauge how you feel
-10 is the worst. +10 is the absolute best.

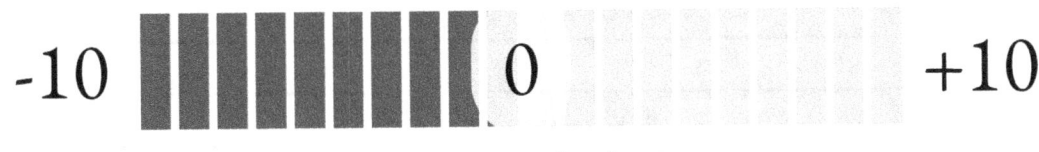

-_____ + Temperature: Freezing - Sweltering

_____
_____
_____
_____

-_____ + Density: Leaden - Weightless

_____
_____
_____
_____

-_____ + Vibration/MPH: Still - Speed of Light

_____
_____
_____
_____

-_____ + Energy: Lethargic - Invigorated

_____
_____
_____
_____

Observations

_____
_____
_____
_____
_____
_____

Self Awareness

Date ____/____/____

In my Mind

_____
_____
_____
_____
_____
_____

In my Heart

_____
_____
_____
_____
_____
_____

From my Soul

_____
_____
_____
_____
_____
_____

Realizations

_____
_____
_____
_____
_____
_____
_____

What I know to be True: Inner Wisdom

Anchoring Intentions

Plan your Weeks. What & How do you need to RECOGNIZE, RELEASE, PROTECT, CONNECT & ACT

Week 1: New Moon

To Recognize

To Release

To Protect

To Connect

To Act

Week 2: Waxing Moon

To Recognize

To Release

To Protect

To Connect

To Act

Week 3: Full Moon

To Recognize

To Release

To Protect

To Connect

To Act

Week 4: Waning Moon

To Recognize

To Release

To Protect

To Connect

To Act

My Priorities

My Wonderful Week ___/___/___

Review your day. What's the takeaway? What are you integrating? What will you invite?

New Moon
Takeaway

Integrating

Invite

Waxing Crescent
Takeaway

Integrating

Invite

Waxing Crescent
Takeaway

Integrating

Invite

Waxing Crescent
Takeaway

Integrating

Invite

Waxing Crescent
Takeaway

Integrating

Invite

Waxing Crescent
Takeaway

Integrating

Invite

Waxing Crescent
Takeaway

Integrating

Invite

My Wonderful Week   ___/___/___

Review your day. What's the takeaway? What are you integrating? What will you invite?

First Quarter
Takeaway

Integrating

Invite

Waxing Gibbous
Takeaway

Integrating

Invite

Waxing Gibbous
Takeaway

Integrating

Invite

Waxing Gibbous
Takeaway

Integrating

Invite

Waxing Gibbous
Takeaway

Integrating

Invite

Waxing Gibbous
Takeaway

Integrating

Invite

Waxing Gibbous
Takeaway

Integrating

Invite

My Wonderful Week   ___/___/___

Review your day. What's the takeaway? What are you integrating? What will you invite?

Full Moon
Takeaway

Integrating

Invite

Waning Gibbous
Takeaway

Integrating

Invite

Waning Gibbous
Takeaway

Integrating

Invite

Waning Gibbous
Takeaway

Integrating

Invite

Waning Gibbous
Takeaway

Integrating

Invite

Waning Gibbous
Takeaway

Integrating

Invite

Waning Gibbous
Takeaway

Integrating

Invite

My Wonderful Week   __ / __ / __

Review your day. What's the takeaway? What are you integrating? What will you invite?

Last Quarter
Takeaway

Integrating

Invite

Waning Crescent
Takeaway

Integrating

Invite

Waning Crescent
Takeaway

Integrating

Invite

Waning Crescent
Takeaway

Integrating

Invite

Waning Crescent
Takeaway

Integrating

Invite

Waning Crescent
Takeaway

Integrating

Invite

Dark Moon
Takeaway

Integrating

Invite

Celebrations & Miracles

Week 1: New Moon
_____
_____
_____
_____

Week 2: Waxing Moon
_____
_____
_____
_____

Week 3: Full Moon
_____
_____
_____
_____

Week 4: Waning Moon
_____
_____
_____
_____

Affirming Statement of Gratitude
_____
_____
_____
_____

Observations & Realizations

Moon 4

I embrace my connection to Divine Source.

As Spirit is always of me and with me, I now welcome my awareness of Holy Presence.

Environment

Date ____/____/____

Smell (close, nearby, faraway)

_____
_____
_____

Sound (close, nearby, faraway)

_____
_____
_____
_____
_____
_____

Sight (close, nearby, faraway)

_____
_____
_____
_____
_____
_____
_____
_____

Touch (Surfaces & Textures around me)

_____
_____
_____

Body Scan

Date ____/____/____

How are your feeling? What are you noticing?

Head & Face

_____
_____
_____
_____

Neck & Shoulders

_____
_____
_____
_____

Spine

_____
_____
_____
_____

Hips & Buttocks

_____
_____
_____
_____

Pelvis & Groin

_____
_____
_____
_____

Chest, Lungs & Heart

_____
_____
_____

Solar Plexus & Belly

_____
_____
_____

Arms & Hands

_____
_____
_____

Legs & Feet

_____
_____
_____

Skin

_____
_____
_____

Additional Notes

_____
_____
_____
_____
_____
_____
_____
_____

Sensation Awareness

Date ———/———/———

Gauge how you feel
-10 is the worst. +10 is the absolute best.

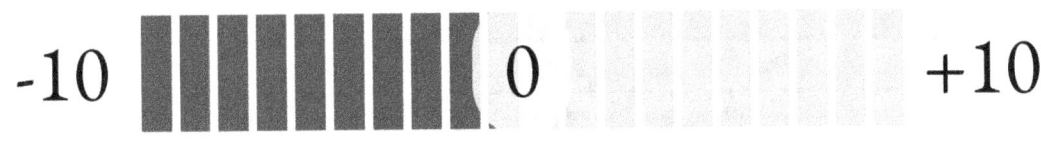

-10   0   +10

-_____ + Temperature: Freezing - Sweltering

_____
_____
_____
_____

-_____ + Density: Leaden - Weightless

_____
_____
_____
_____

-_____ + Vibration/MPH: Still - Speed of Light

_____
_____
_____
_____

-_____ + Energy: Lethargic - Invigorated

_____
_____
_____
_____

Observations

_____
_____
_____
_____
_____

Self Awareness

Date ____/____/____

In my Mind

In my Heart

From my Soul

Realizations

What I know to be True: Inner Wisdom

Anchoring Intentions

Plan your Weeks. What & How do you need to RECOGNIZE, RELEASE, PROTECT, CONNECT & ACT

Week 1: New Moon

To Recognize

To Release

To Protect

To Connect

To Act

Week 2: Waxing Moon

To Recognize

To Release

To Protect

To Connect

To Act

Week 3: Full Moon

To Recognize

To Release

To Protect

To Connect

To Act

Week 4: Waning Moon

To Recognize

To Release

To Protect

To Connect

To Act

My Priorities

My Wonderful Week   ___/___/___

Review your day. What's the takeaway? What are you integrating? What will you invite?

New Moon
Takeaway

Integrating

Invite

Waxing Crescent
Takeaway

Integrating

Invite

Waxing Crescent
Takeaway

Integrating

Invite

Waxing Crescent
Takeaway

Integrating

Invite

Waxing Crescent
Takeaway

Integrating

Invite

Waxing Crescent
Takeaway

Integrating

Invite

Waxing Crescent
Takeaway

Integrating

Invite

My Wonderful Week   ___ / ___ / ___

Review your day. What's the takeaway? What are you integrating? What will you invite?

First Quarter
Takeaway

Integrating

Invite

Waxing Gibbous
Takeaway

Integrating

Invite

Waxing Gibbous
Takeaway

Integrating

Invite

Waxing Gibbous
Takeaway

Integrating

Invite

Waxing Gibbous
Takeaway

Integrating

Invite

Waxing Gibbous
Takeaway

Integrating

Invite

Waxing Gibbous
Takeaway

Integrating

Invite

My Wonderful Week   ___/___/___

Review your day. What's the takeaway? What are you integrating? What will you invite?

Full Moon
Takeaway

Integrating

Invite

Waning Gibbous
Takeaway

Integrating

Invite

Waning Gibbous
Takeaway

Integrating

Invite

Waning Gibbous
Takeaway

Integrating

Invite

Waning Gibbous
Takeaway

Integrating

Invite

Waning Gibbous
Takeaway

Integrating

Invite

Waning Gibbous
Takeaway

Integrating

Invite

My Wonderful Week   ___/___/___

Review your day. What's the takeaway? What are you integrating? What will you invite?

Last Quarter
Takeaway

Integrating

Invite

Waning Crescent
Takeaway

Integrating

Invite

Waning Crescent
Takeaway

Integrating

Invite

Waning Crescent
Takeaway

Integrating

Invite

Waning Crescent
Takeaway

Integrating

Invite

Waning Crescent
Takeaway

Integrating

Invite

Dark Moon
Takeaway

Integrating

Invite

Celebrations & Miracles

Week 1: New Moon

_____
_____
_____
_____

Week 2: Waxing Moon

_____
_____
_____
_____

Week 3: Full Moon

_____
_____
_____
_____

Week 4: Waning Moon

_____
_____
_____
_____

Affirming Statement of Gratitude

_____
_____
_____
_____

Observations & Realizations

Moon 5

I embrace the choices and actions that sustain my strength and safety.

I serve my purpose with Grace and Ease.

Environment

Date ——/——/——

Smell (close, nearby, faraway)

_____
_____
_____

Sound (close, nearby, faraway)

_____
_____
_____
_____
_____
_____
_____

Sight (close, nearby, faraway)

_____
_____
_____
_____
_____
_____
_____

Touch (Surfaces & Textures around me)

_____
_____
_____

Body Scan

Date ___/___/___

How are your feeling? What are you noticing?

Head & Face

_____
_____
_____
_____

Neck & Shoulders

_____
_____
_____
_____

Spine

_____
_____
_____
_____

Hips & Buttocks

_____
_____
_____
_____

Pelvis & Groin

_____
_____
_____
_____

Chest, Lungs & Heart

_____
_____
_____
_____

Solar Plexus & Belly

_____
_____
_____
_____

Arms & Hands

_____
_____
_____
_____

Legs & Feet

_____
_____
_____
_____

Skin

_____
_____
_____
_____

Additional Notes

_____
_____
_____
_____
_____
_____
_____
_____

Sensation Awareness

Date ____/____/____

Gauge how you feel
-10 is the worst. +10 is the absolute best.

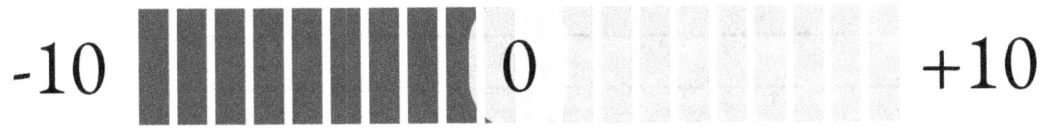

-10   0   +10

-_____ + Temperature: Freezing - Sweltering

_____
_____
_____
_____

-_____ + Density: Leaden - Weightless

_____
_____
_____
_____

-_____ + Vibration/MPH: Still - Speed of Light

_____
_____
_____
_____

-_____ + Energy: Lethargic - Invigorated

_____
_____
_____
_____

Observations

_____
_____
_____
_____
_____

Self Awareness

Date ____/____/____

In my Mind

In my Heart

From my Soul

Realizations

What I know to be True: Inner Wisdom

Anchoring Intentions

Plan your Weeks. What & How do you need to RECOGNIZE, RELEASE, PROTECT, CONNECT & ACT

Week 1: New Moon

To Recognize

To Release

To Protect

To Connect

To Act

Week 2: Waxing Moon

To Recognize

To Release

To Protect

To Connect

To Act

Week 3: Full Moon

To Recognize

To Release

To Protect

To Connect

To Act

Week 4: Waning Moon

To Recognize

To Release

To Protect

To Connect

To Act

My Priorities

My Wonderful Week   ___/___/___

Review your day. What's the takeaway? What are you integrating? What will you invite?

New Moon
Takeaway

Integrating

Invite

Waxing Crescent
Takeaway

Integrating

Invite

Waxing Crescent
Takeaway

Integrating

Invite

Waxing Crescent
Takeaway

Integrating

Invite

Waxing Crescent
Takeaway

Integrating

Invite

Waxing Crescent
Takeaway

Integrating

Invite

Waxing Crescent
Takeaway

Integrating

Invite

My Wonderful Week ___/___/___

Review your day. What's the takeaway? What are you integrating? What will you invite?

First Quarter
Takeaway

Integrating

Invite

Waxing Gibbous
Takeaway

Integrating

Invite

Waxing Gibbous
Takeaway

Integrating

Invite

Waxing Gibbous
Takeaway

Integrating

Invite

Waxing Gibbous
Takeaway

Integrating

Invite

Waxing Gibbous
Takeaway

Integrating

Invite

Waxing Gibbous
Takeaway

Integrating

Invite

My Wonderful Week   ___/___/___

Review your day. What's the takeaway? What are you integrating? What will you invite?

Full Moon
Takeaway

Integrating

Invite

Waning Gibbous
Takeaway

Integrating

Invite

Waning Gibbous
Takeaway

Integrating

Invite

Waning Gibbous
Takeaway

Integrating

Invite

Waning Gibbous
Takeaway

Integrating

Invite

Waning Gibbous
Takeaway

Integrating

Invite

Waning Gibbous
Takeaway

Integrating

Invite

My Wonderful Week   ___/___/___

Review your day. What's the takeaway? What are you integrating? What will you invite?

Last Quarter
Takeaway

Integrating

Invite

Waning Crescent
Takeaway

Integrating

Invite

Waning Crescent
Takeaway

Integrating

Invite

Waning Crescent
Takeaway

Integrating

Invite

Waning Crescent
Takeaway

Integrating

Invite

Waning Crescent
Takeaway

Integrating

Invite

Dark Moon
Takeaway

Integrating

Invite

Celebrations & Miracles

Week 1: New Moon
_____
_____
_____
_____

Week 2: Waxing Moon
_____
_____
_____
_____

Week 3: Full Moon
_____
_____
_____

Week 4: Waning Moon
_____
_____
_____
_____

Affirming Statement of Gratitude
_____
_____
_____

Observations & Realizations

Moon 6

I support myself and others to grow beyond our limitations and to claim a truly magnificent life.

I turn my attention to delight and abundance.

Environment

Date ——/——/——

Smell (close, nearby, faraway)

Sound (close, nearby, faraway)

Sight (close, nearby, faraway)

Touch (Surfaces & Textures around me)

Body Scan

Date ____/____/____

How are your feeling? What are you noticing?

Head & Face

Chest, Lungs & Heart

Neck & Shoulders

Solar Plexus & Belly

Spine

Arms & Hands

Hips & Buttocks

Legs & Feet

Pelvis & Groin

Skin

Additional Notes

Sensation Awareness

Date ——/——/——

Gauge how you feel
-10 is the worst. +10 is the absolute best.

-10 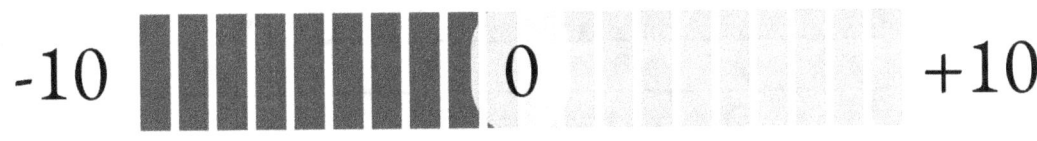 0 +10

-_____ + Temperature: Freezing - Sweltering

_____
_____
_____
_____

-_____ + Density: Leaden - Weightless

_____
_____
_____
_____

-_____ + Vibration/MPH: Still - Speed of Light

_____
_____
_____
_____

-_____ + Energy: Lethargic - Invigorated

_____
_____
_____
_____

Observations
_____
_____
_____
_____
_____

Self Awareness

Date ____/____/____

In my Mind

In my Heart

From my Soul

Realizations

What I know to be True: Inner Wisdom

Anchoring Intentions

Plan your Weeks. What & How do you need to RECOGNIZE, RELEASE, PROTECT, CONNECT & ACT

Week 1: New Moon

To Recognize

To Release

To Protect

To Connect

To Act

Week 2: Waxing Moon

To Recognize

To Release

To Protect

To Connect

To Act

Week 3: Full Moon

To Recognize

To Release

To Protect

To Connect

To Act

Week 4: Waning Moon

To Recognize

To Release

To Protect

To Connect

To Act

My Priorities

My Wonderful Week ___/___/___

Review your day. What's the takeaway? What are you integrating? What will you invite?

New Moon
Takeaway

Integrating

Invite

Waxing Crescent
Takeaway

Integrating

Invite

Waxing Crescent
Takeaway

Integrating

Invite

Waxing Crescent
Takeaway

Integrating

Invite

Waxing Crescent
Takeaway

Integrating

Invite

Waxing Crescent
Takeaway

Integrating

Invite

Waxing Crescent
Takeaway

Integrating

Invite

My Wonderful Week   ___/___/___

Review your day. What's the takeaway? What are you integrating? What will you invite?

First Quarter
Takeaway

Integrating

Invite

Waxing Gibbous
Takeaway

Integrating

Invite

Waxing Gibbous
Takeaway

Integrating

Invite

Waxing Gibbous
Takeaway

Integrating

Invite

Waxing Gibbous
Takeaway

Integrating

Invite

Waxing Gibbous
Takeaway

Integrating

Invite

Waxing Gibbous
Takeaway

Integrating

Invite

My Wonderful Week   __/__/__

Review your day. What's the takeaway? What are you integrating? What will you invite?

Full Moon
Takeaway

Integrating

Invite

Waning Gibbous
Takeaway

Integrating

Invite

Waning Gibbous
Takeaway

Integrating

Invite

Waning Gibbous
Takeaway

Integrating

Invite

Waning Gibbous
Takeaway

Integrating

Invite

Waning Gibbous
Takeaway

Integrating

Invite

Waning Gibbous
Takeaway

Integrating

Invite

My Wonderful Week   ___/___/___

Review your day. What's the takeaway? What are you integrating? What will you invite?

Last Quarter
Takeaway

Integrating

Invite

Waning Crescent
Takeaway

Integrating

Invite

Waning Crescent
Takeaway

Integrating

Invite

Waning Crescent
Takeaway

Integrating

Invite

Waning Crescent
Takeaway

Integrating

Invite

Waning Crescent
Takeaway

Integrating

Invite

Dark Moon
Takeaway

Integrating

Invite

Celebrations & Miracles

Week 1: New Moon

_____
_____
_____
_____

Week 2: Waxing Moon

_____
_____
_____
_____

Week 3: Full Moon

_____
_____
_____
_____

Week 4: Waning Moon

_____
_____
_____
_____

Affirming Statement of Gratitude

_____
_____
_____

Observations & Realizations

Moon 7

I choose to relax and trust that good things are on their way.

It's only a matter of time before my deepest heart's desire manifests.

Body Scan

Date ____/____/____

How are your feeling? What are you noticing?

Head & Face

_____
_____
_____

Neck & Shoulders

_____
_____
_____

Spine

_____
_____
_____

Hips & Buttocks

_____
_____
_____

Pelvis & Groin

_____
_____
_____

Chest, Lungs & Heart

_____
_____
_____

Solar Plexus & Belly

_____
_____
_____

Arms & Hands

_____
_____
_____

Legs & Feet

_____
_____
_____

Skin

_____
_____
_____

Additional Notes

_____
_____
_____
_____
_____
_____
_____
_____

Sensation Awareness

Date ____/____/____

Gauge how you feel
-10 is the worst. +10 is the absolute best.

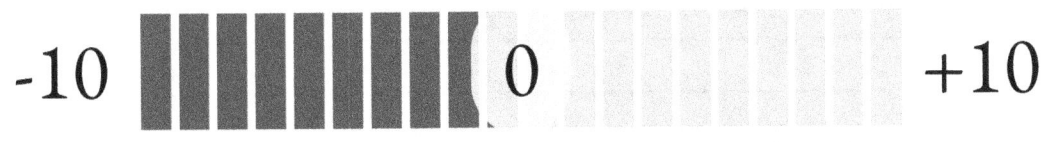

-_____ + **Temperature: Freezing - Sweltering**

_____
_____
_____
_____

-_____ + **Density: Leaden - Weightless**

_____
_____
_____
_____

-_____ + **Vibration/MPH: Still - Speed of Light**

_____
_____
_____
_____

-_____ + **Energy: Lethargic - Invigorated**

_____
_____
_____
_____

Observations

_____
_____
_____
_____
_____

Self Awareness

Date ——/——/——

In my Mind

In my Heart

From my Soul

Realizations

What I know to be True: Inner Wisdom

Anchoring Intentions

Plan your Weeks. What & How do you need to RECOGNIZE, RELEASE, PROTECT, CONNECT & ACT

Week 1: New Moon

To Recognize

To Release

To Protect

To Connect

To Act

Week 2: Waxing Moon

To Recognize

To Release

To Protect

To Connect

To Act

Week 3: Full Moon

To Recognize

To Release

To Protect

To Connect

To Act

Week 4: Waning Moon

To Recognize

To Release

To Protect

To Connect

To Act

My Priorities

My Wonderful Week   ___/___/___

Review your day. What's the takeaway? What are you integrating? What will you invite?

New Moon
Takeaway

Integrating

Invite

Waxing Crescent
Takeaway

Integrating

Invite

Waxing Crescent
Takeaway

Integrating

Invite

Waxing Crescent
Takeaway

Integrating

Invite

Waxing Crescent
Takeaway

Integrating

Invite

Waxing Crescent
Takeaway

Integrating

Invite

Waxing Crescent
Takeaway

Integrating

Invite

My Wonderful Week   ___/___/___

Review your day. What's the takeaway? What are you integrating? What will you invite?

First Quarter
Takeaway
Integrating
Invite

Waxing Gibbous
Takeaway
Integrating
Invite

Waxing Gibbous
Takeaway
Integrating
Invite

Waxing Gibbous
Takeaway
Integrating
Invite

Waxing Gibbous
Takeaway
Integrating
Invite

Waxing Gibbous
Takeaway
Integrating
Invite

Waxing Gibbous
Takeaway
Integrating
Invite

My Wonderful Week   ___/___/___

Review your day. What's the takeaway? What are you integrating? What will you invite?

Full Moon

Takeaway

Integrating

Invite

Waning Gibbous

Takeaway

Integrating

Invite

Waning Gibbous

Takeaway

Integrating

Invite

Waning Gibbous

Takeaway

Integrating

Invite

Waning Gibbous

Takeaway

Integrating

Invite

Waning Gibbous

Takeaway

Integrating

Invite

Waning Gibbous

Takeaway

Integrating

Invite

My Wonderful Week   ___/___/___

Review your day. What's the takeaway? What are you integrating? What will you invite?

Last Quarter
Takeaway

Integrating

Invite

Waning Crescent
Takeaway

Integrating

Invite

Waning Crescent
Takeaway

Integrating

Invite

Waning Crescent
Takeaway

Integrating

Invite

Waning Crescent
Takeaway

Integrating

Invite

Waning Crescent
Takeaway

Integrating

Invite

Dark Moon
Takeaway

Integrating

Invite

Celebrations & Miracles

Week 1: New Moon

Week 2: Waxing Moon

Week 3: Full Moon

Week 4: Waning Moon

Affirming Statement of Gratitude

Observations & Realizations

Moon 8

I offer what I can when it's appropriate and healthy for me.

I only share with those who truly value and appreciate my unique gifts.

Environment

Date ____/____/____

Smell (close, nearby, faraway)

_____
_____
_____

Sound (close, nearby, faraway)

_____
_____
_____
_____
_____
_____
_____

Sight (close, nearby, faraway)

_____
_____
_____
_____
_____
_____
_____
_____

Touch (Surfaces & Textures around me)

_____
_____
_____
_____

Body Scan

Date ____/____/____

How are your feeling? What are you noticing?

Head & Face	Chest, Lungs & Heart

Neck & Shoulders	Solar Plexus & Belly

Spine	Arms & Hands

Hips & Buttocks	Legs & Feet

Pelvis & Groin	Skin

Additional Notes

Sensation Awareness

Date ____/____/____

Gauge how you feel
-10 is the worst. +10 is the absolute best.

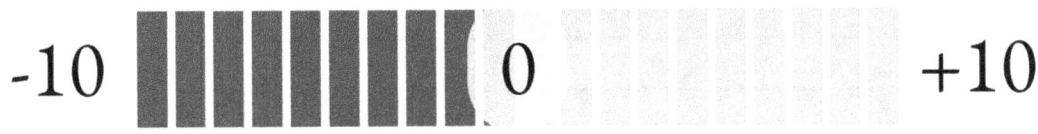

-_____ + Temperature: Freezing - Sweltering

_____
_____
_____

-_____ + Density: Leaden - Weightless

_____
_____
_____

-_____ + Vibration/MPH: Still - Speed of Light

_____
_____
_____

-_____ + Energy: Lethargic - Invigorated

_____
_____
_____

Observations
_____
_____
_____
_____
_____

Self Awareness

Date ____/____/____

In my Mind

___

In my Heart

___

From my Soul

___

Realizations

___

What I know to be True: Inner Wisdom

Anchoring Intentions

Plan your Weeks. What & How do you need to RECOGNIZE, RELEASE, PROTECT, CONNECT & ACT

Week 1: New Moon

To Recognize

To Release

To Protect

To Connect

To Act

Week 2: Waxing Moon

To Recognize

To Release

To Protect

To Connect

To Act

Week 3: Full Moon

To Recognize

To Release

To Protect

To Connect

To Act

Week 4: Waning Moon

To Recognize

To Release

To Protect

To Connect

To Act

My Priorities

My Wonderful Week   ___/___/___

Review your day. What's the takeaway? What are you integrating? What will you invite?

New Moon
Takeaway

Integrating

Invite

Waxing Crescent
Takeaway

Integrating

Invite

Waxing Crescent
Takeaway

Integrating

Invite

Waxing Crescent
Takeaway

Integrating

Invite

Waxing Crescent
Takeaway

Integrating

Invite

Waxing Crescent
Takeaway

Integrating

Invite

Waxing Crescent
Takeaway

Integrating

Invite

My Wonderful Week

___ / ___ / ___

Review your day. What's the takeaway? What are you integrating? What will you invite?

First Quarter
Takeaway
Integrating
Invite

Waxing Gibbous
Takeaway
Integrating
Invite

Waxing Gibbous
Takeaway
Integrating
Invite

Waxing Gibbous
Takeaway
Integrating
Invite

Waxing Gibbous
Takeaway
Integrating
Invite

Waxing Gibbous
Takeaway
Integrating
Invite

Waxing Gibbous
Takeaway
Integrating
Invite

My Wonderful Week ___/___/___

Review your day. What's the takeaway? What are you integrating? What will you invite?

Full Moon
Takeaway

Integrating

Invite

Waning Gibbous
Takeaway

Integrating

Invite

Waning Gibbous
Takeaway

Integrating

Invite

Waning Gibbous
Takeaway

Integrating

Invite

Waning Gibbous
Takeaway

Integrating

Invite

Waning Gibbous
Takeaway

Integrating

Invite

Waning Gibbous
Takeaway

Integrating

Invite

My Wonderful Week   ___/___/___

Review your day. What's the takeaway? What are you integrating? What will you invite?

Last Quarter
Takeaway

Integrating

Invite

Waning Crescent
Takeaway

Integrating

Invite

Waning Crescent
Takeaway

Integrating

Invite

Waning Crescent
Takeaway

Integrating

Invite

Waning Crescent
Takeaway

Integrating

Invite

Waning Crescent
Takeaway

Integrating

Invite

Dark Moon
Takeaway

Integrating

Invite

Celebrations & Miracles

Week 1: New Moon

Week 2: Waxing Moon

Week 3: Full Moon

Week 4: Waning Moon

Affirming Statement of Gratitude

Observations & Realizations

Moon 9

I acknowledge and appreciate the blessings and abundance unfolding in my life today.

I embrace all miracles, large and small.

Environment

Date ——/——/——

Smell (close, nearby, faraway)

_____
_____
_____

Sound (close, nearby, faraway)

_____
_____
_____
_____
_____
_____
_____

Sight (close, nearby, faraway)

_____
_____
_____
_____
_____
_____
_____
_____
_____

Touch (Surfaces & Textures around me)

_____
_____
_____
_____

Body Scan

Date ____/____/____

How are your feeling? What are you noticing?

Head & Face

_____
_____
_____

Neck & Shoulders

_____
_____
_____

Spine

_____
_____
_____

Hips & Buttocks

_____
_____
_____

Pelvis & Groin

_____
_____
_____

Chest, Lungs & Heart

_____
_____
_____

Solar Plexus & Belly

_____
_____
_____

Arms & Hands

_____
_____
_____

Legs & Feet

_____
_____
_____

Skin

_____
_____
_____

Additional Notes

_____
_____
_____
_____
_____
_____
_____
_____

Sensation Awareness

Date ____/____/____

Gauge how you feel
-10 is the worst. +10 is the absolute best.

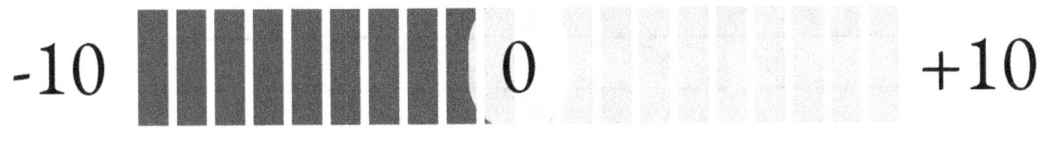

-10   0   +10

-_____ + **Temperature: Freezing - Sweltering**

_____
_____
_____
_____

-_____ + **Density: Leaden - Weightless**

_____
_____
_____
_____

-_____ + **Vibration/MPH: Still - Speed of Light**

_____
_____
_____
_____

-_____ + **Energy: Lethargic - Invigorated**

_____
_____
_____
_____

Observations
_____
_____
_____
_____

Self Awareness

Date ———/———/———

In my Mind

In my Heart

From my Soul

Realizations

What I know to be True: Inner Wisdom

Anchoring Intentions

Plan your Weeks. What & How do you need to RECOGNIZE, RELEASE, PROTECT, CONNECT & ACT

Week 1: New Moon

To Recognize

To Release

To Protect

To Connect

To Act

Week 2: Waxing Moon

To Recognize

To Release

To Protect

To Connect

To Act

Week 3: Full Moon

To Recognize

To Release

To Protect

To Connect

To Act

Week 4: Waning Moon

To Recognize

To Release

To Protect

To Connect

To Act

My Priorities

My Wonderful Week   ___/___/___

Review your day. What's the takeaway? What are you integrating? What will you invite?

New Moon
Takeaway

Integrating

Invite

Waxing Crescent
Takeaway

Integrating

Invite

Waxing Crescent
Takeaway

Integrating

Invite

Waxing Crescent
Takeaway

Integrating

Invite

Waxing Crescent
Takeaway

Integrating

Invite

Waxing Crescent
Takeaway

Integrating

Invite

Waxing Crescent
Takeaway

Integrating

Invite

My Wonderful Week   ___/___/___

Review your day. What's the takeaway? What are you integrating? What will you invite?

First Quarter
Takeaway

Integrating

Invite

Waxing Gibbous
Takeaway

Integrating

Invite

Waxing Gibbous
Takeaway

Integrating

Invite

Waxing Gibbous
Takeaway

Integrating

Invite

Waxing Gibbous
Takeaway

Integrating

Invite

Waxing Gibbous
Takeaway

Integrating

Invite

Waxing Gibbous
Takeaway

Integrating

Invite

My Wonderful Week   ___/___/___

Review your day. What's the takeaway? What are you integrating? What will you invite?

Full Moon
Takeaway

Integrating

Invite

Waning Gibbous
Takeaway

Integrating

Invite

Waning Gibbous
Takeaway

Integrating

Invite

Waning Gibbous
Takeaway

Integrating

Invite

Waning Gibbous
Takeaway

Integrating

Invite

Waning Gibbous
Takeaway

Integrating

Invite

Waning Gibbous
Takeaway

Integrating

Invite

My Wonderful Week   ___/___/___

Review your day. What's the takeaway? What are you integrating? What will you invite?

Last Quarter
Takeaway

Integrating

Invite

Waning Crescent
Takeaway

Integrating

Invite

Waning Crescent
Takeaway

Integrating

Invite

Waning Crescent
Takeaway

Integrating

Invite

Waning Crescent
Takeaway

Integrating

Invite

Waning Crescent
Takeaway

Integrating

Invite

Dark Moon
Takeaway

Integrating

Invite

Celebrations & Miracles

Week 1: New Moon

_____
_____
_____
_____

Week 2: Waxing Moon

_____
_____
_____
_____

Week 3: Full Moon

_____
_____
_____
_____

Week 4: Waning Moon

_____
_____
_____
_____

Affirming Statement of Gratitude

_____
_____
_____

Observations & Realizations

Moon 10

I honor the struggles of the ancestors who came before me.

I use my skills, resources and wisdom to help set things right.

Environment

Date ——/——/——

Smell (close, nearby, faraway)

_____
_____
_____

Sound (close, nearby, faraway)

_____
_____
_____
_____
_____
_____
_____

Sight (close, nearby, faraway)

_____
_____
_____
_____
_____
_____
_____
_____
_____

Touch (Surfaces & Textures around me)

_____
_____
_____
_____

Body Scan

Date ___/___/___

How are you feeling? What are you noticing?

Head & Face

Neck & Shoulders

Spine

Hips & Buttocks

Pelvis & Groin

Chest, Lungs & Heart

Solar Plexus & Belly

Arms & Hands

Legs & Feet

Skin

Additional Notes

Sensation Awareness

Date ____/____/____

Gauge how you feel
-10 is the worst. +10 is the absolute best.

-10 |||||||||| 0 |||||||||| +10

-_____ + Temperature: Freezing - Sweltering

_____
_____
_____
_____

-_____ + Density: Leaden - Weightless

_____
_____
_____
_____

-_____ + Vibration/MPH: Still - Speed of Light

_____
_____
_____
_____

-_____ + Energy: Lethargic - Invigorated

_____
_____
_____
_____

Observations
_____
_____
_____
_____
_____
_____

Self Awareness

Date ___/___/___

In my Mind

_____
_____
_____
_____
_____
_____

In my Heart

_____
_____
_____
_____
_____
_____

From my Soul

_____
_____
_____
_____
_____
_____

Realizations

_____
_____
_____
_____
_____
_____
_____
_____

What I know to be True: Inner Wisdom

Anchoring Intentions

Plan your Weeks. What & How do you need to RECOGNIZE, RELEASE, PROTECT, CONNECT & ACT

Week 1: New Moon

To Recognize

To Release

To Protect

To Connect

To Act

Week 2: Waxing Moon

To Recognize

To Release

To Protect

To Connect

To Act

Week 3: Full Moon

To Recognize

To Release

To Protect

To Connect

To Act

Week 4: Waning Moon

To Recognize

To Release

To Protect

To Connect

To Act

My Priorities

My Wonderful Week ___/___/___

Review your day. What's the takeaway? What are you integrating? What will you invite?

New Moon
Takeaway

Integrating

Invite

Waxing Crescent
Takeaway

Integrating

Invite

Waxing Crescent
Takeaway

Integrating

Invite

Waxing Crescent
Takeaway

Integrating

Invite

Waxing Crescent
Takeaway

Integrating

Invite

Waxing Crescent
Takeaway

Integrating

Invite

Waxing Crescent
Takeaway

Integrating

Invite

My Wonderful Week ___/___/___

Review your day. What's the takeaway? What are you integrating? What will you invite?

First Quarter
Takeaway

Integrating

Invite

Waxing Gibbous
Takeaway

Integrating

Invite

Waxing Gibbous
Takeaway

Integrating

Invite

Waxing Gibbous
Takeaway

Integrating

Invite

Waxing Gibbous
Takeaway

Integrating

Invite

Waxing Gibbous
Takeaway

Integrating

Invite

Waxing Gibbous
Takeaway

Integrating

Invite

My Wonderful Week   ___/___/___

Review your day. What's the takeaway? What are you integrating? What will you invite?

Full Moon
Takeaway

Integrating

Invite

Waning Gibbous
Takeaway

Integrating

Invite

Waning Gibbous
Takeaway

Integrating

Invite

Waning Gibbous
Takeaway

Integrating

Invite

Waning Gibbous
Takeaway

Integrating

Invite

Waning Gibbous
Takeaway

Integrating

Invite

Waning Gibbous
Takeaway

Integrating

Invite

My Wonderful Week   ___/___/___

Review your day. What's the takeaway? What are you integrating? What will you invite?

Last Quarter
Takeaway

Integrating

Invite

Waning Crescent
Takeaway

Integrating

Invite

Waning Crescent
Takeaway

Integrating

Invite

Waning Crescent
Takeaway

Integrating

Invite

Waning Crescent
Takeaway

Integrating

Invite

Waning Crescent
Takeaway

Integrating

Invite

Dark Moon
Takeaway

Integrating

Invite

Celebrations & Miracles

Week 1: New Moon

_____
_____
_____
_____

Week 2: Waxing Moon

_____
_____
_____
_____

Week 3: Full Moon

_____
_____
_____
_____

Week 4: Waning Moon

_____
_____
_____
_____

Affirming Statement of Gratitude

_____
_____
_____

Observations & Realizations

Moon 11

It's totally okay for me to rest and recharge.

I show up and work hard. I deserve to relax and play.

Environment

Date ——/——/——

Smell (close, nearby, faraway)

_____
_____
_____

Sound (close, nearby, faraway)

_____
_____
_____
_____
_____
_____
_____

Sight (close, nearby, faraway)

_____
_____
_____
_____
_____
_____
_____
_____

Touch (Surfaces & Textures around me)

_____
_____
_____
_____

Body Scan

Date ____/____/____

How are your feeling? What are you noticing?

Head & Face

_____
_____
_____

Neck & Shoulders

_____
_____
_____

Spine

_____
_____
_____

Hips & Buttocks

_____
_____
_____

Pelvis & Groin

_____
_____
_____

Chest, Lungs & Heart

_____
_____
_____

Solar Plexus & Belly

_____
_____
_____

Arms & Hands

_____
_____
_____

Legs & Feet

_____
_____
_____

Skin

_____
_____
_____

Additional Notes

_____
_____
_____
_____
_____
_____
_____
_____

Sensation Awareness

Date ____/____/____

Gauge how you feel
-10 is the worst. +10 is the absolute best.

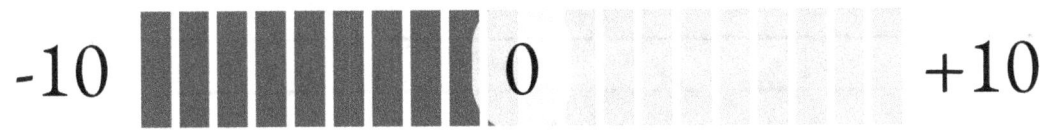

-10   0   +10

-_____ + Temperature: Freezing - Sweltering

_____
_____
_____

-_____ + Density: Leaden - Weightless

_____
_____
_____

-_____ + Vibration/MPH: Still - Speed of Light

_____
_____
_____

-_____ + Energy: Lethargic - Invigorated

_____
_____
_____

Observations
_____
_____
_____
_____

Self Awareness

Date ____/____/____

In my Mind

_____
_____
_____
_____
_____
_____

In my Heart

_____
_____
_____
_____
_____
_____

From my Soul

_____
_____
_____
_____
_____
_____

Realizations

_____
_____
_____
_____
_____
_____
_____

What I know to be True: Inner Wisdom

Anchoring Intentions

Plan your Weeks. What & How do you need to RECOGNIZE, RELEASE, PROTECT, CONNECT & ACT

Week 1: New Moon

To Recognize

To Release

To Protect

To Connect

To Act

Week 2: Waxing Moon

To Recognize

To Release

To Protect

To Connect

To Act

Week 3: Full Moon

To Recognize

To Release

To Protect

To Connect

To Act

Week 4: Waning Moon

To Recognize

To Release

To Protect

To Connect

To Act

My Priorities

My Wonderful Week   __/__/__

Review your day. What's the takeaway? What are you integrating? What will you invite?

New Moon
Takeaway

Integrating

Invite

Waxing Crescent
Takeaway

Integrating

Invite

Waxing Crescent
Takeaway

Integrating

Invite

Waxing Crescent
Takeaway

Integrating

Invite

Waxing Crescent
Takeaway

Integrating

Invite

Waxing Crescent
Takeaway

Integrating

Invite

Waxing Crescent
Takeaway

Integrating

Invite

My Wonderful Week   ___/___/___

Review your day. What's the takeaway? What are you integrating? What will you invite?

First Quarter
Takeaway

Integrating

Invite

Waxing Gibbous
Takeaway

Integrating

Invite

Waxing Gibbous
Takeaway

Integrating

Invite

Waxing Gibbous
Takeaway

Integrating

Invite

Waxing Gibbous
Takeaway

Integrating

Invite

Waxing Gibbous
Takeaway

Integrating

Invite

Waxing Gibbous
Takeaway

Integrating

Invite

My Wonderful Week   ___/___/___

Review your day. What's the takeaway? What are you integrating? What will you invite?

Full Moon
Takeaway

Integrating

Invite

Waning Gibbous
Takeaway

Integrating

Invite

Waning Gibbous
Takeaway

Integrating

Invite

Waning Gibbous
Takeaway

Integrating

Invite

Waning Gibbous
Takeaway

Integrating

Invite

Waning Gibbous
Takeaway

Integrating

Invite

Waning Gibbous
Takeaway

Integrating

Invite

My Wonderful Week   ___/___/___

Review your day. What's the takeaway? What are you integrating? What will you invite?

Last Quarter
Takeaway

Integrating

Invite

Waning Crescent
Takeaway

Integrating

Invite

Waning Crescent
Takeaway

Integrating

Invite

Waning Crescent
Takeaway

Integrating

Invite

Waning Crescent
Takeaway

Integrating

Invite

Waning Crescent
Takeaway

Integrating

Invite

Dark Moon
Takeaway

Integrating

Invite

Celebrations & Miracles

Week 1: New Moon

_____
_____
_____
_____

Week 2: Waxing Moon

_____
_____
_____
_____

Week 3: Full Moon

_____
_____
_____
_____

Week 4: Waning Moon

_____
_____
_____
_____

Affirming Statement of Gratitude

_____
_____
_____

Observations & Realizations

Moon 12

I witness other's concerns with love and compassion.

It's okay for me to release all the burdens I've carried for anyone else.

Environment

Date ——/——/——

Smell (close, nearby, faraway)

_____
_____
_____
_____

Sound (close, nearby, faraway)

_____
_____
_____
_____
_____
_____
_____
_____

Sight (close, nearby, faraway)

_____
_____
_____
_____
_____
_____
_____
_____
_____
_____

Touch (Surfaces & Textures around me)

_____
_____
_____

Body Scan

Date ___/___/___

How are your feeling? What are you noticing?

Head & Face

Chest, Lungs & Heart

Neck & Shoulders

Solar Plexus & Belly

Spine

Arms & Hands

Hips & Buttocks

Legs & Feet

Pelvis & Groin

Skin

Additional Notes

Sensation Awareness

Date ____/____/____

Gauge how you feel
-10 is the worst. +10 is the absolute best.

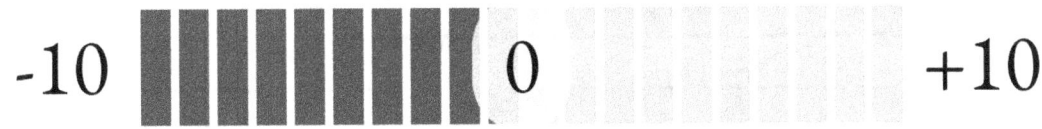

-10   0   +10

-_____+ Temperature: Freezing - Sweltering

_____
_____
_____
_____

-_____+ Density: Leaden - Weightless

_____
_____
_____
_____

-_____+ Vibration/MPH: Still - Speed of Light

_____
_____
_____
_____

-_____+ Energy: Lethargic - Invigorated

_____
_____
_____
_____

Observations

_____
_____
_____
_____
_____

Self Awareness

Date ____/____/____

In my Mind

In my Heart

From my Soul

Realizations

What I know to be True: Inner Wisdom

Anchoring Intentions

Plan your Weeks. What & How do you need to RECOGNIZE, RELEASE, PROTECT, CONNECT & ACT

Week 1: New Moon

To Recognize

To Release

To Protect

To Connect

To Act

Week 2: Waxing Moon

To Recognize

To Release

To Protect

To Connect

To Act

Week 3: Full Moon

To Recognize

To Release

To Protect

To Connect

To Act

Week 4: Waning Moon

To Recognize

To Release

To Protect

To Connect

To Act

My Priorities

My Wonderful Week ___/___/___

Review your day. What's the takeaway? What are you integrating? What will you invite?

New Moon
Takeaway

Integrating

Invite

Waxing Crescent
Takeaway

Integrating

Invite

Waxing Crescent
Takeaway

Integrating

Invite

Waxing Crescent
Takeaway

Integrating

Invite

Waxing Crescent
Takeaway

Integrating

Invite

Waxing Crescent
Takeaway

Integrating

Invite

Waxing Crescent
Takeaway

Integrating

Invite

My Wonderful Week

___/___/___

Review your day. What's the takeaway? What are you integrating? What will you invite?

First Quarter
Takeaway

Integrating

Invite

Waxing Gibbous
Takeaway

Integrating

Invite

Waxing Gibbous
Takeaway

Integrating

Invite

Waxing Gibbous
Takeaway

Integrating

Invite

Waxing Gibbous
Takeaway

Integrating

Invite

Waxing Gibbous
Takeaway

Integrating

Invite

Waxing Gibbous
Takeaway

Integrating

Invite

My Wonderful Week   ___/___/___

Review your day. What's the takeaway? What are you integrating? What will you invite?

Full Moon
Takeaway

Integrating

Invite

Waning Gibbous
Takeaway

Integrating

Invite

Waning Gibbous
Takeaway

Integrating

Invite

Waning Gibbous
Takeaway

Integrating

Invite

Waning Gibbous
Takeaway

Integrating

Invite

Waning Gibbous
Takeaway

Integrating

Invite

Waning Gibbous
Takeaway

Integrating

Invite

My Wonderful Week

_____/_____/_____

Review your day. What's the takeaway? What are you integrating? What will you invite?

Last Quarter

Takeaway

Integrating

Invite

Waning Crescent

Takeaway

Integrating

Invite

Waning Crescent

Takeaway

Integrating

Invite

Waning Crescent

Takeaway

Integrating

Invite

Waning Crescent

Takeaway

Integrating

Invite

Waning Crescent

Takeaway

Integrating

Invite

Dark Moon

Takeaway

Integrating

Invite

Celebrations & Miracles

Week 1: New Moon

_____
_____
_____
_____

Week 2: Waxing Moon

_____
_____
_____
_____

Week 3: Full Moon

_____
_____
_____
_____

Week 4: Waning Moon

_____
_____
_____
_____

Affirming Statement of Gratitude

_____
_____
_____
_____

Observations & Realizations

Moon 13

I celebrate the growth I've achieved and the discoveries I've made.

I deserve to claim every small victory and moment of joy.

Environment

Date ——/——/——

Smell (close, nearby, faraway)

_____
_____
_____

Sound (close, nearby, faraway)

_____
_____
_____
_____
_____
_____
_____

Sight (close, nearby, faraway)

_____
_____
_____
_____
_____
_____
_____
_____
_____

Touch (Surfaces & Textures around me)

_____
_____
_____
_____

Body Scan

Date ____/____/____

How are your feeling? What are you noticing?

Head & Face
_____
_____
_____

Neck & Shoulders
_____
_____
_____

Spine
_____
_____
_____

Hips & Buttocks
_____
_____
_____

Pelvis & Groin
_____
_____
_____

Chest, Lungs & Heart
_____
_____
_____

Solar Plexus & Belly
_____
_____
_____

Arms & Hands
_____
_____
_____

Legs & Feet
_____
_____
_____

Skin
_____
_____
_____

Additional Notes

_____
_____
_____
_____
_____
_____
_____

Sensation Awareness

Date ____/____/____

Gauge how you feel
-10 is the worst. +10 is the absolute best.

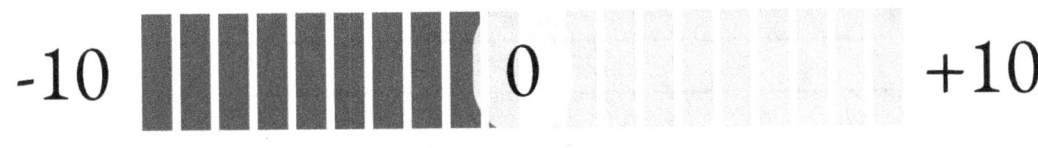

-10   0   +10

-_____ + Temperature: Freezing - Sweltering

_____
_____
_____
_____

-_____ + Density: Leaden - Weightless

_____
_____
_____
_____

-_____ + Vibration/MPH: Still - Speed of Light

_____
_____
_____
_____

-_____ + Energy: Lethargic - Invigorated

_____
_____
_____
_____

Observations
_____
_____
_____
_____
_____

Self Awareness

Date ____/____/____

In my Mind

_____
_____
_____
_____
_____
_____

In my Heart

_____
_____
_____
_____
_____
_____

From my Soul

_____
_____
_____
_____
_____
_____

Realizations

_____
_____
_____
_____
_____
_____
_____

What I Know to be True: Inner Wisdom

Anchoring Intentions

Plan your Weeks. What & How do you need to RECOGNIZE, RELEASE, PROTECT, CONNECT & ACT

Week 1: New Moon

To Recognize

To Release

To Protect

To Connect

To Act

Week 2: Waxing Moon

To Recognize

To Release

To Protect

To Connect

To Act

Week 3: Full Moon

To Recognize

To Release

To Protect

To Connect

To Act

Week 4: Waning Moon

To Recognize

To Release

To Protect

To Connect

To Act

My Priorities

My Wonderful Week ___/___/___

Review your day. What's the takeaway? What are you integrating? What will you invite?

New Moon
Takeaway

Integrating

Invite

Waxing Crescent
Takeaway

Integrating

Invite

Waxing Crescent
Takeaway

Integrating

Invite

Waxing Crescent
Takeaway

Integrating

Invite

Waxing Crescent
Takeaway

Integrating

Invite

Waxing Crescent
Takeaway

Integrating

Invite

Waxing Crescent
Takeaway

Integrating

Invite

My Wonderful Week   ____/____/____

Review your day. What's the takeaway? What are you integrating? What will you invite?

First Quarter
Takeaway

Integrating

Invite

Waxing Gibbous
Takeaway

Integrating

Invite

Waxing Gibbous
Takeaway

Integrating

Invite

Waxing Gibbous
Takeaway

Integrating

Invite

Waxing Gibbous
Takeaway

Integrating

Invite

Waxing Gibbous
Takeaway

Integrating

Invite

Waxing Gibbous
Takeaway

Integrating

Invite

My Wonderful Week ____/____/____

Review your day. What's the takeaway? What are you integrating? What will you invite?

Full Moon
Takeaway

Integrating

Invite

Waning Gibbous
Takeaway

Integrating

Invite

Waning Gibbous
Takeaway

Integrating

Invite

Waning Gibbous
Takeaway

Integrating

Invite

Waning Gibbous
Takeaway

Integrating

Invite

Waning Gibbous
Takeaway

Integrating

Invite

Waning Gibbous
Takeaway

Integrating

Invite

My Wonderful Week   ___/___/___

Review your day. What's the takeaway? What are you integrating? What will you invite?

Last Quarter
Takeaway

Integrating

Invite

Waning Crescent
Takeaway

Integrating

Invite

Waning Crescent
Takeaway

Integrating

Invite

Waning Crescent
Takeaway

Integrating

Invite

Waning Crescent
Takeaway

Integrating

Invite

Waning Crescent
Takeaway

Integrating

Invite

Dark Moon
Takeaway

Integrating

Invite

Celebrations & Miracles

Week 1: New Moon

___
___
___
___

Week 2: Waxing Moon

___
___
___
___

Week 3: Full Moon

___
___
___
___

Week 4: Waning Moon

___
___
___
___

Affirming Statement of Gratitude

___
___
___

Observations & Realizations

Completion

Appreciating My Victories & Shifts

Final Assessment

Gauge how you feel
-10 is the worst. +10 is the absolute best.

-10 ▮▮▮▮▮▮▮▮ 0 ▯▯▯▯▯▯▯▯ +10

1. Physical Wellbeing _____
2. Mental Wellbeing _____
3. Emotional Wellbeing _____
4. Spiritual Wellbeing _____
5. Alignment with Divine Source _____
6. Sleep & Relaxation _____
7. Sensitivities or Allergies _____
8. Financial Security _____
9. Confidence & Success _____
10. Vitality & Drive _____
11. Creative Expression _____
12. Intimate Relationships _____
13. Energetic Filters & Shields _____
14. Strategic Boundaries _____
15. Overwhelm _____
16. Taking On Other People's Thoughts/Feelings _____
17. Attraction to/from Wounded People _____
18. Urgent Need to Rescue _____
19. Awfulizing _____
20. Awareness of Ghosts & Spirits _____
21. Past Life Trauma _____
22. Ancestral Trauma _____

Total Score_____

My Victories

My Shifts

My Lessons

My Hopes for Next Year

Notes

Divine Source

Grant me the Grace
To receive your Grace
and
Show me the Beauty Way

and Please
Grant me the willingness
To be willing
To walk that way as it is
Revealed

-- amen

A Special Gift for You

After working with these principles of Empathic Mastery, I sincerely hope you're feeling more calm, centered and empowered. My goal in writing my book, Empathic Mastery, and creating this diary was to offer new ways for you to understand and utilize your empathic sensitivity so that it can actually serve you and those you love.

Therefore, I've created an additional gift for you to add to your tool kit. It's my Empathic Safety Kit. It's packed with additional content, including an Earth/Sky Connection Meditation and Body Scan audio recordings, EFT/Tapping videos, and more resources that will support you in taking your abilities to the next level.

You can claim your Empathic Safety Kit for free at: EmpathicSafety.com The sooner you learn to manage your sensitivity, the easier it becomes to be a channel for peace and healing even in the midst of chaos.

I'd love to be in your corner. Please feel free to reach out and let me know if I can help further. Here's to your Empathic Mastery!

Visit EmpathicSafety.com

Big Big Gratitude

Before you turn this final page and close the cover, I want to express my deepest thanks to you for buying (and using) this diary. AND I have a simple request: I'll be over the moon for you to post a sincere review on Amazon, Good Reads, and/or wherever you purchased your copy.

Reviews are beyond priceless for an indie author like me. AND fortunately it's one of the easiest and most effective ways you can help this work reach more people who need it.

It only takes a few minutes to write a line or two sharing your biggest takeaways and results from using this guide. ★★★★★ Your honest review is gold. It helps more than you might imagine.

Please visit EmpathicMastery.com/diary Or visit: Your favorite book platform and search in books for "*Empathic Mastery Diary*" by Jennifer Elizabeth Moore.
I can assure you, you'll make my week. Thank you in advance for helping me and supporting the Empathic Mastery Diary so it can thrive!